This Book Belongs To:

....

Cars & Trucks

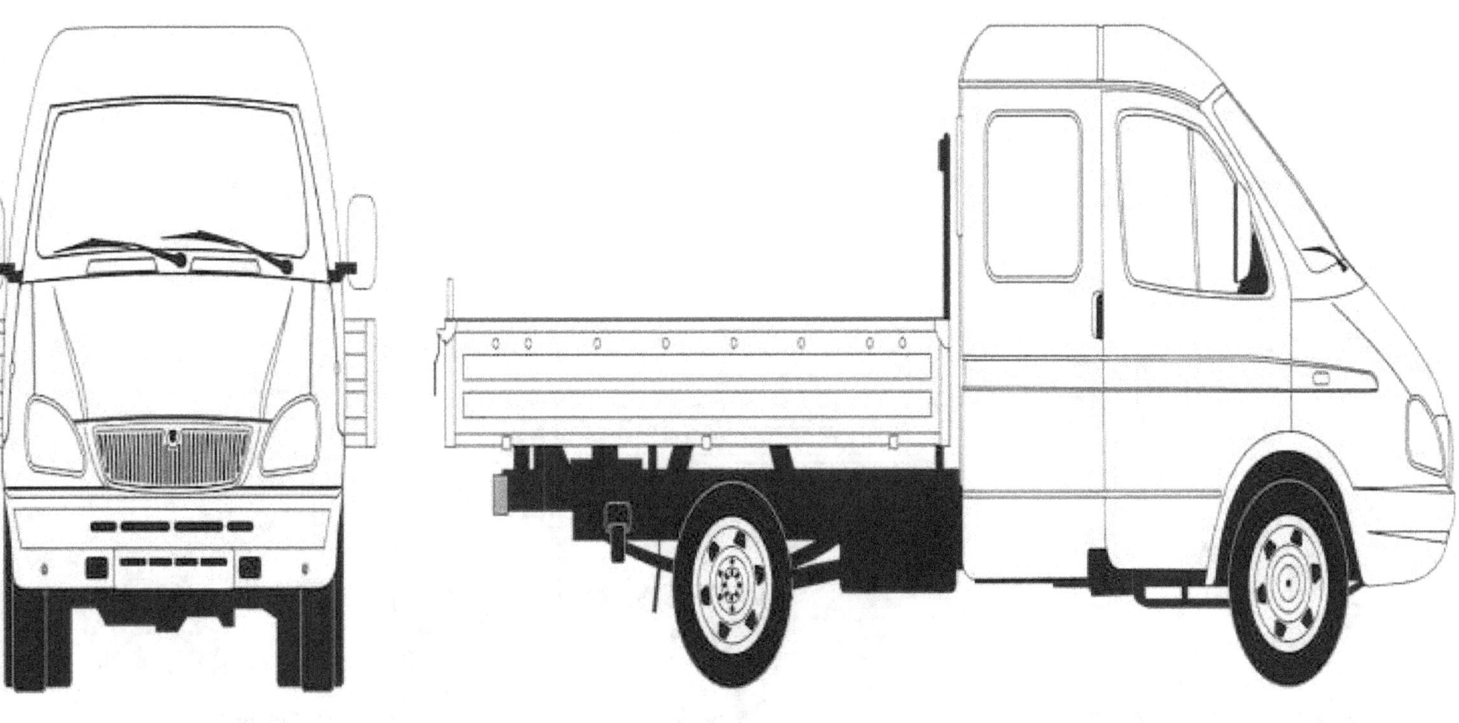

Bus

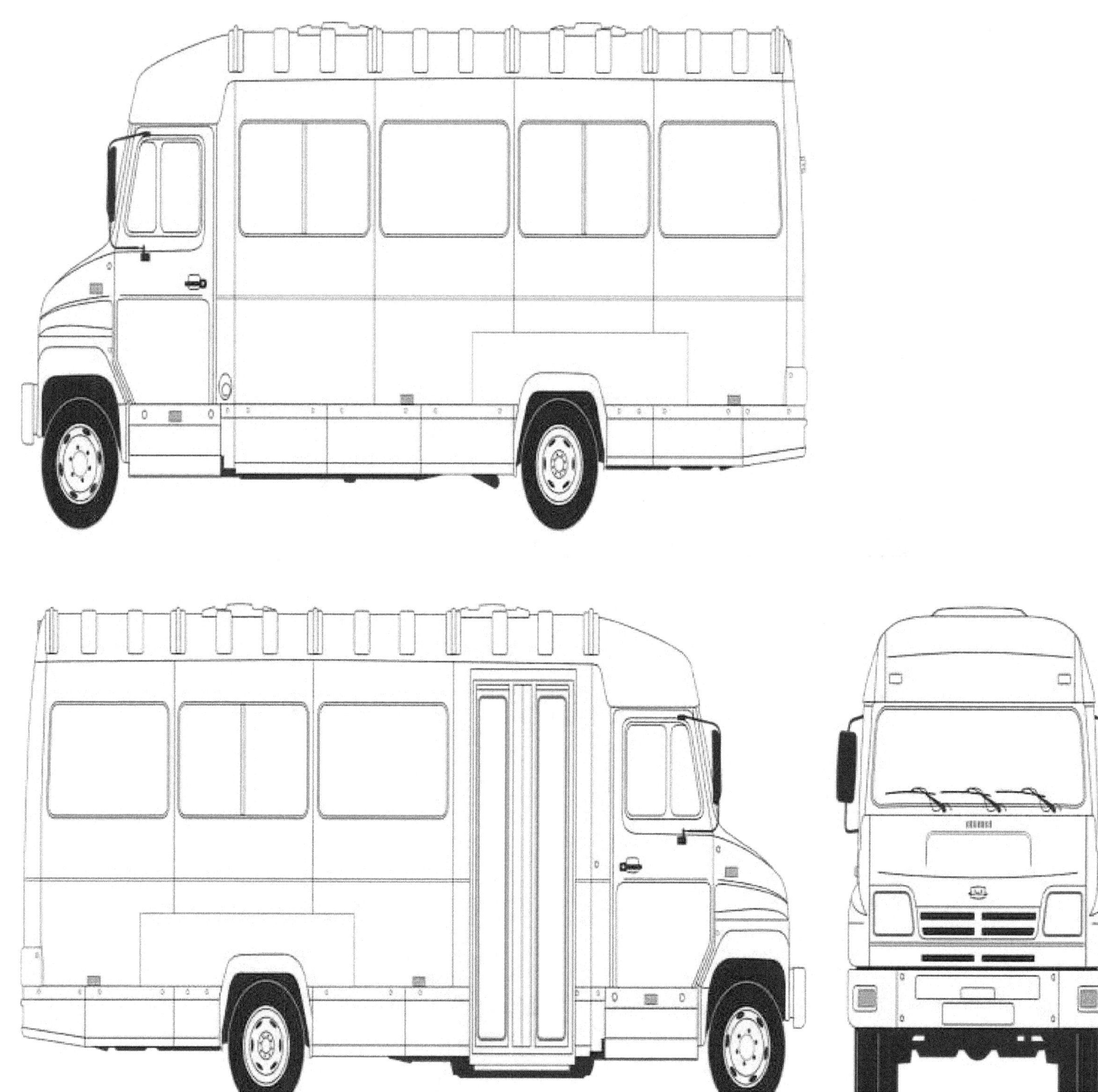

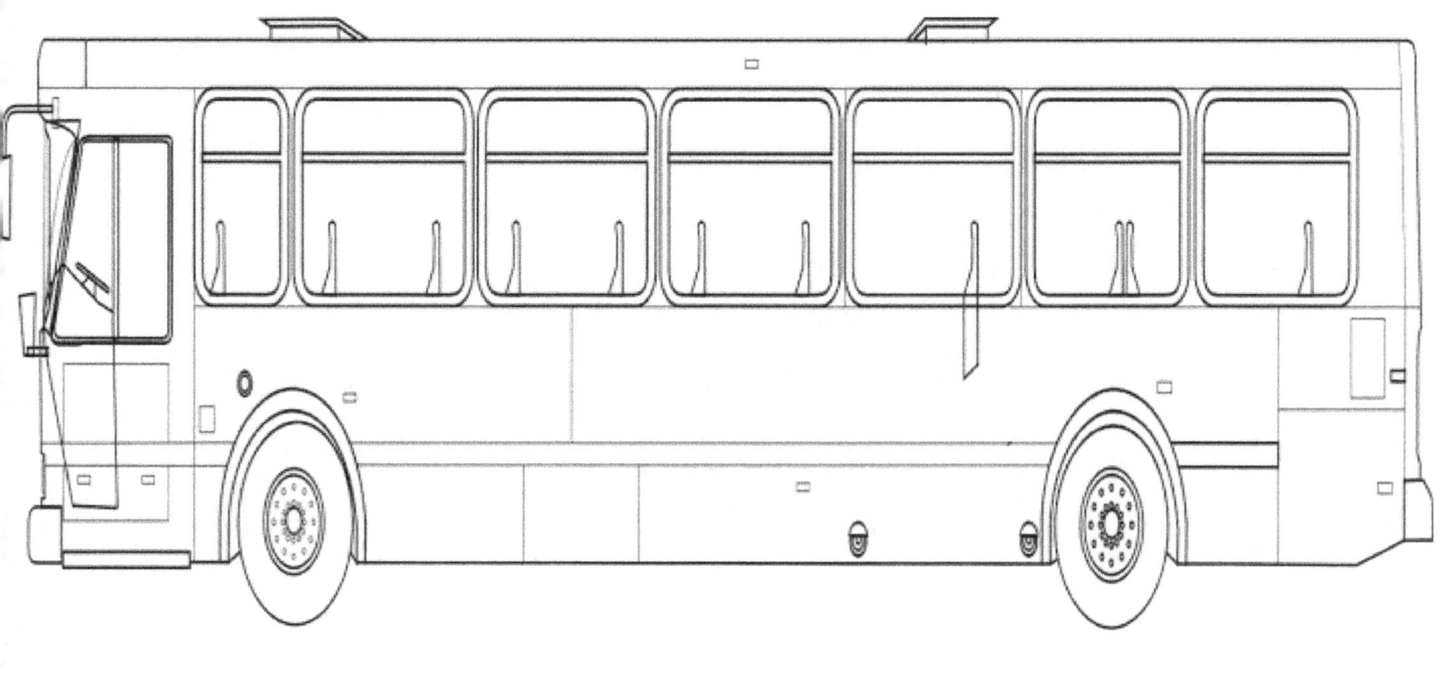

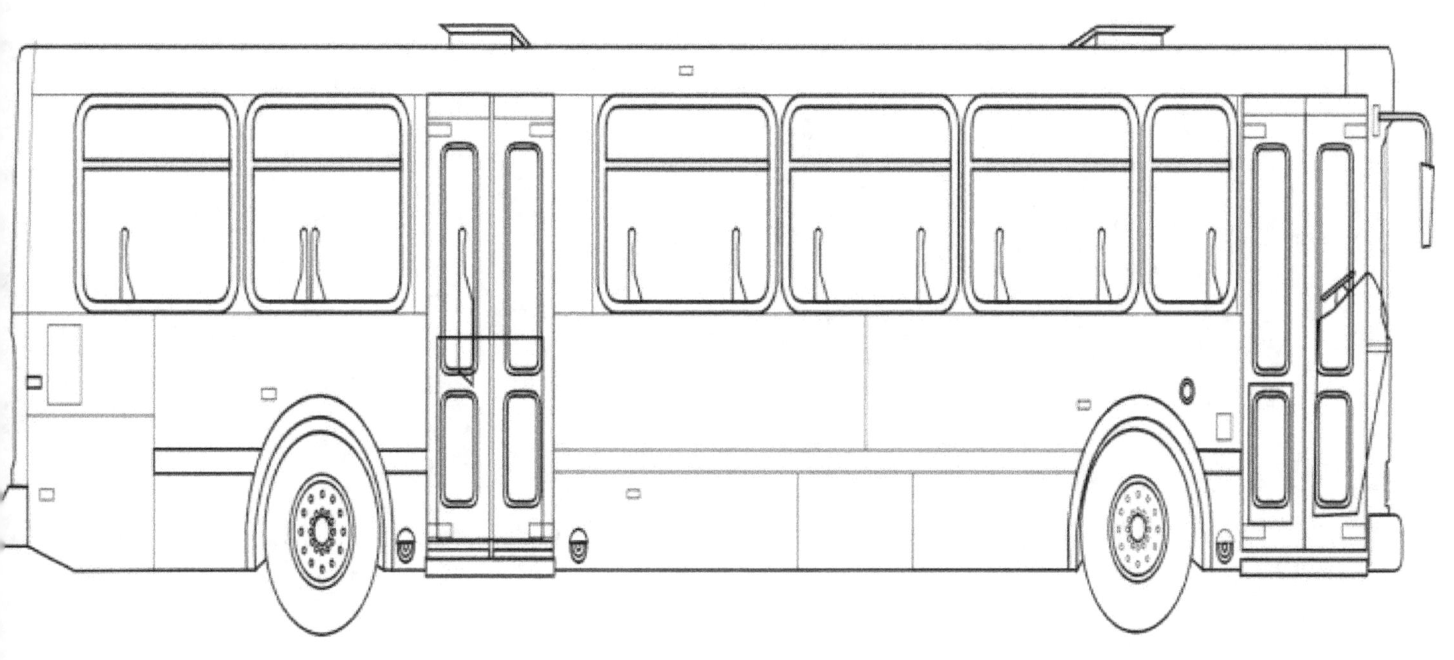

Fire Truck

AMBULANCE

Trains

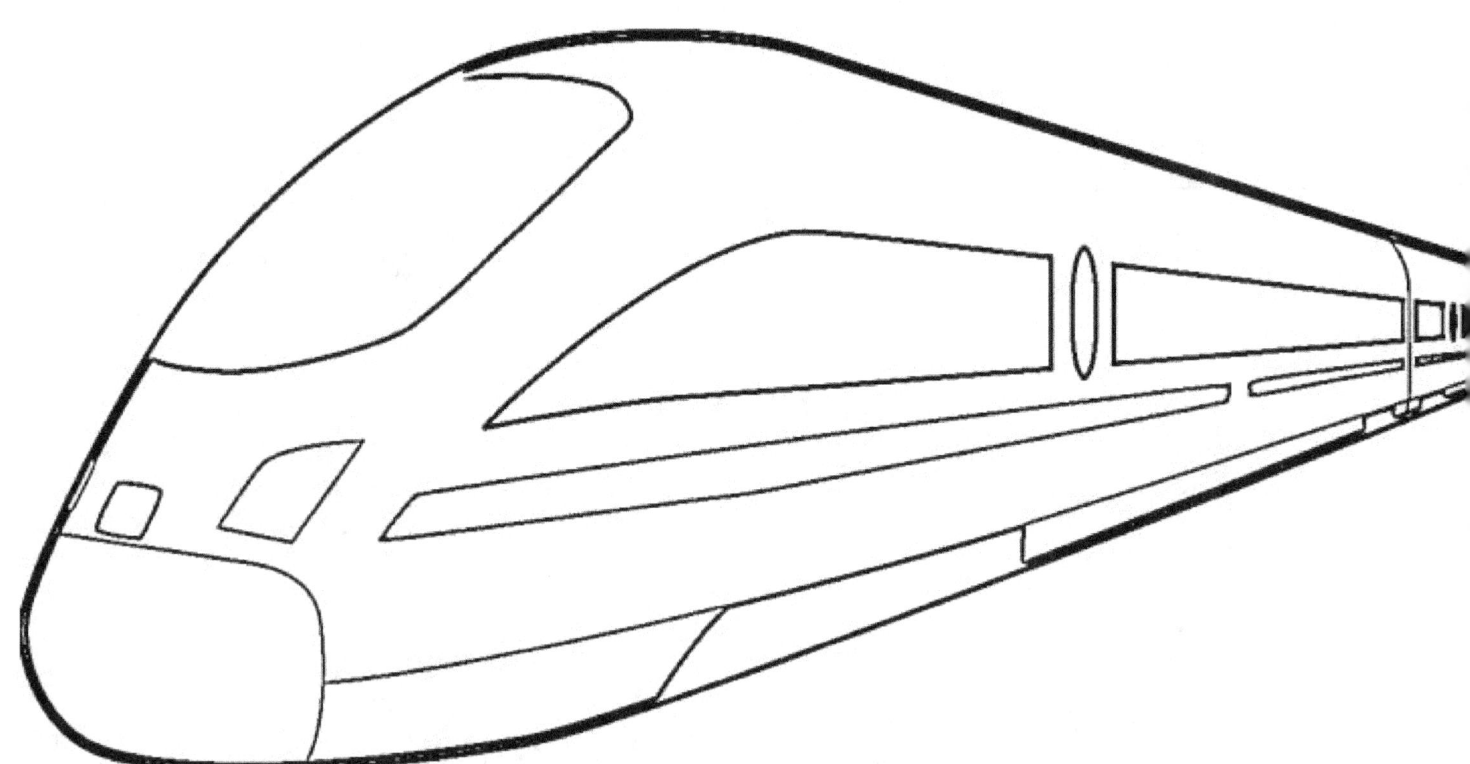

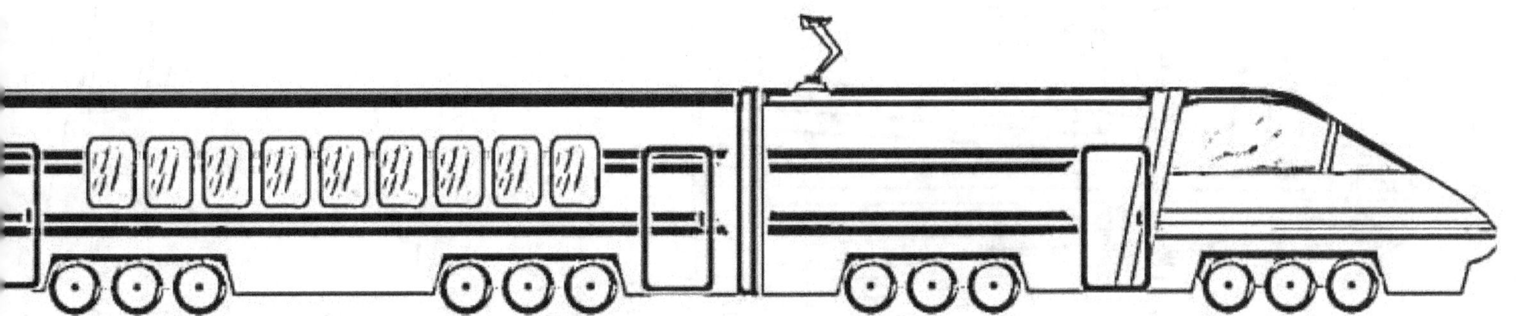

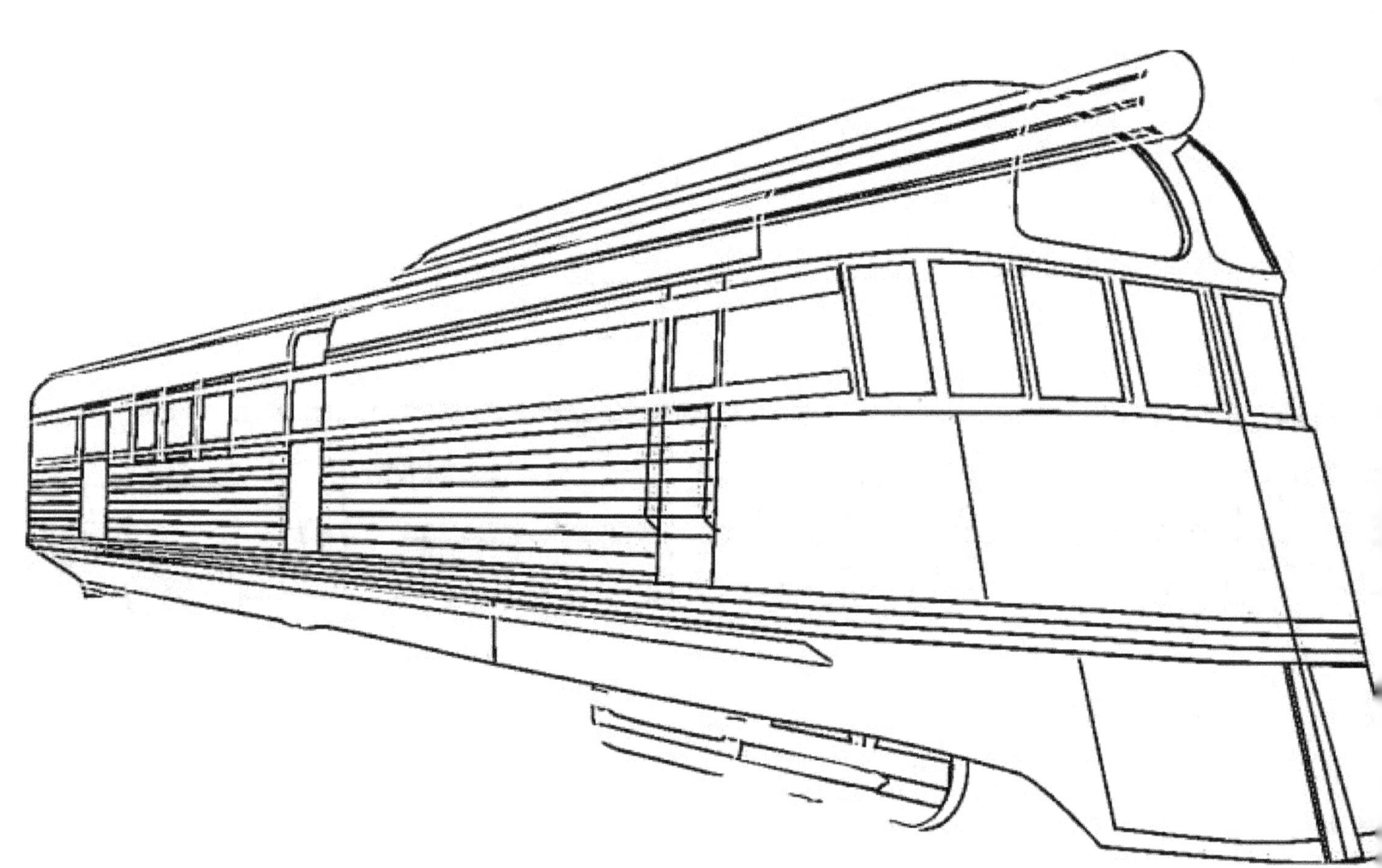

上野・東京方面
JR

AirPlanes

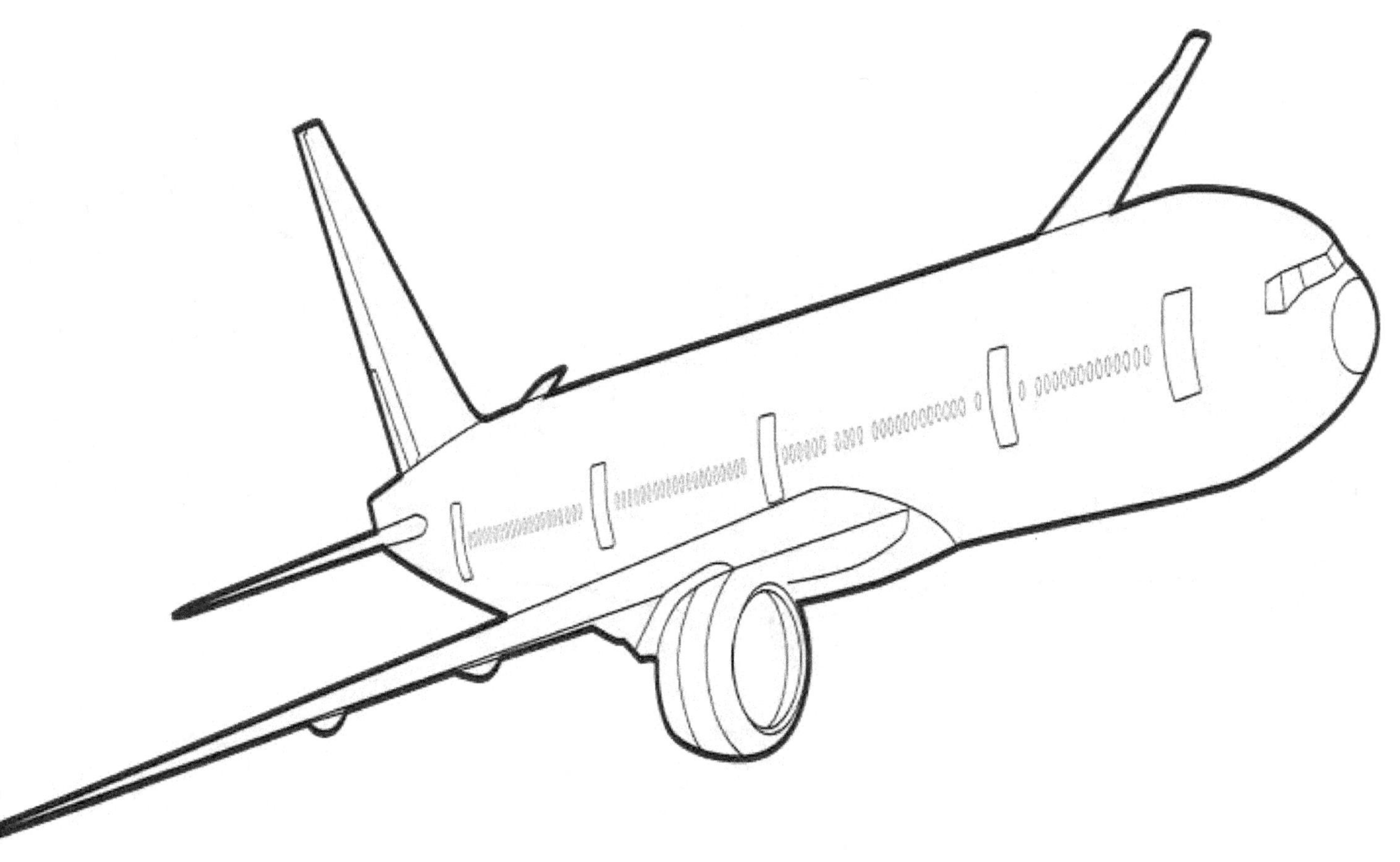

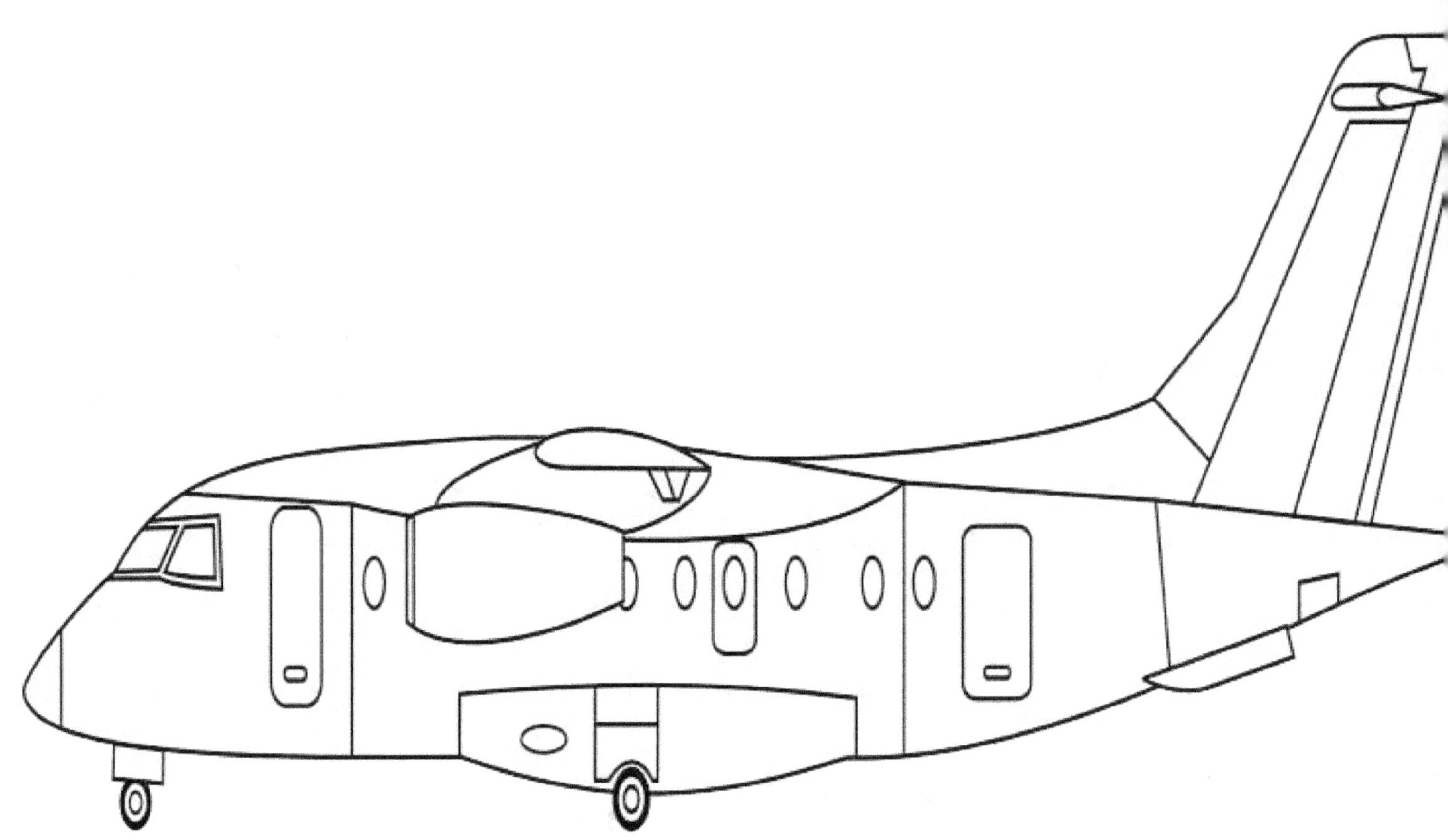

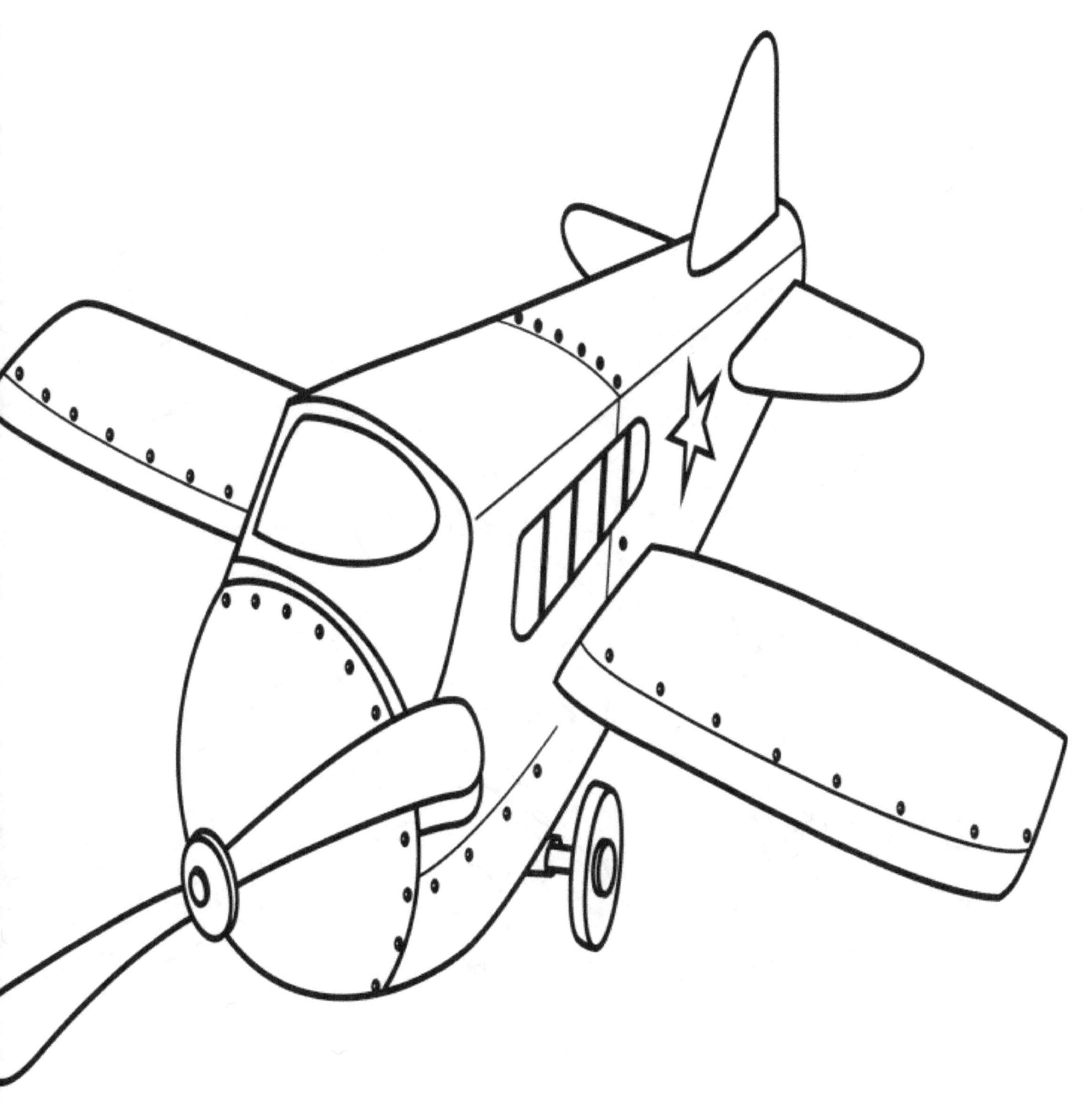

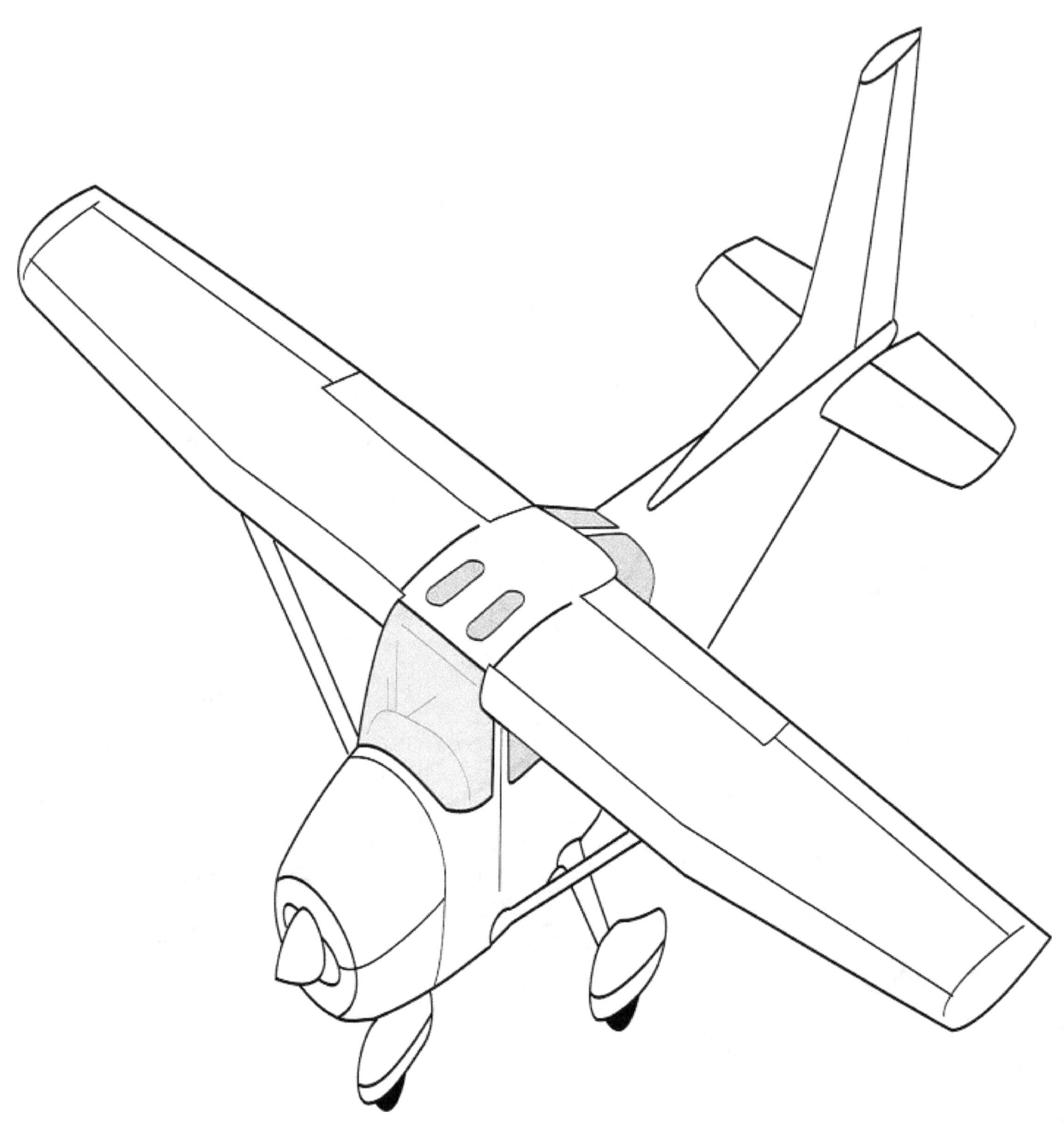

AirShip

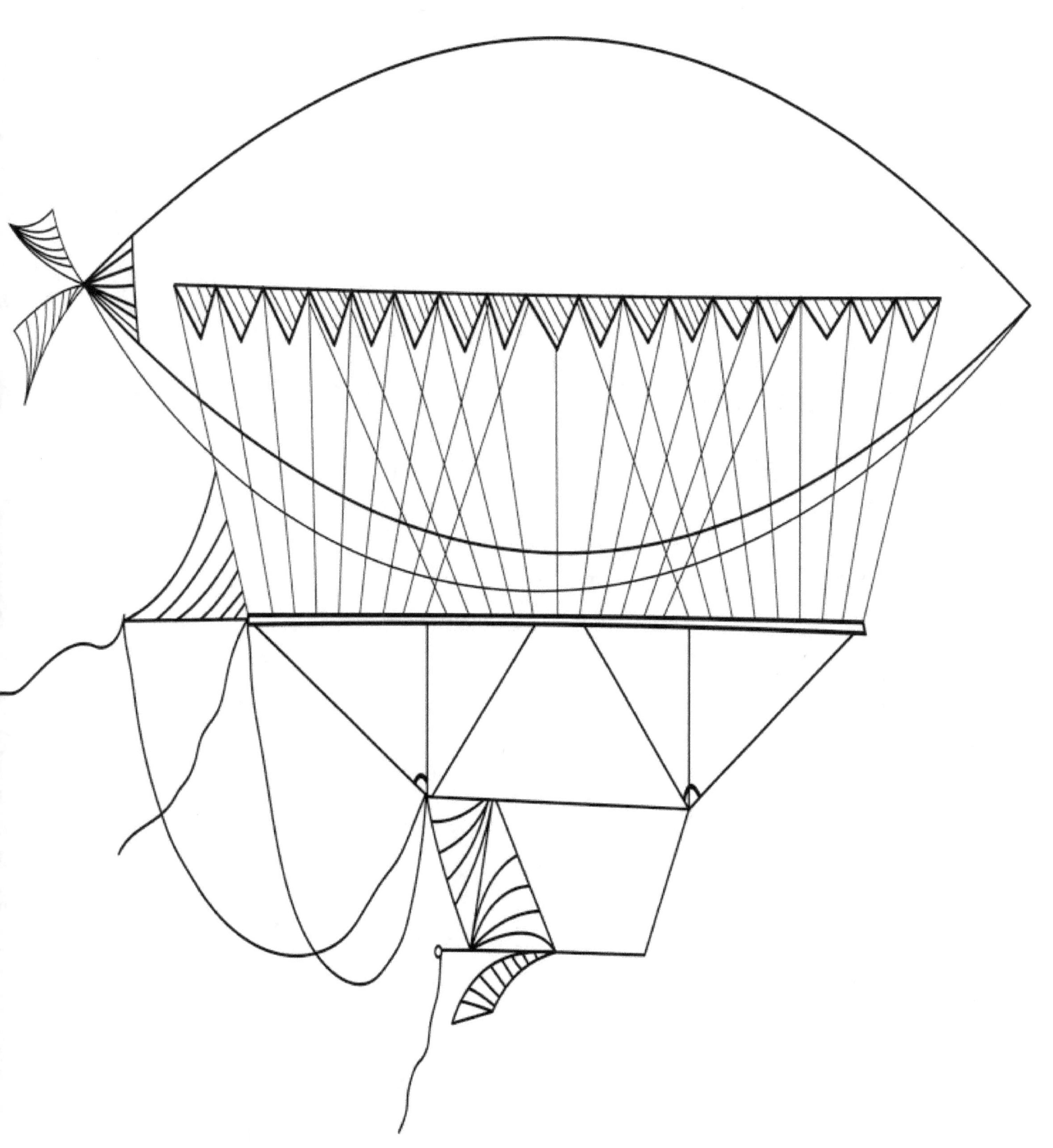

Boats

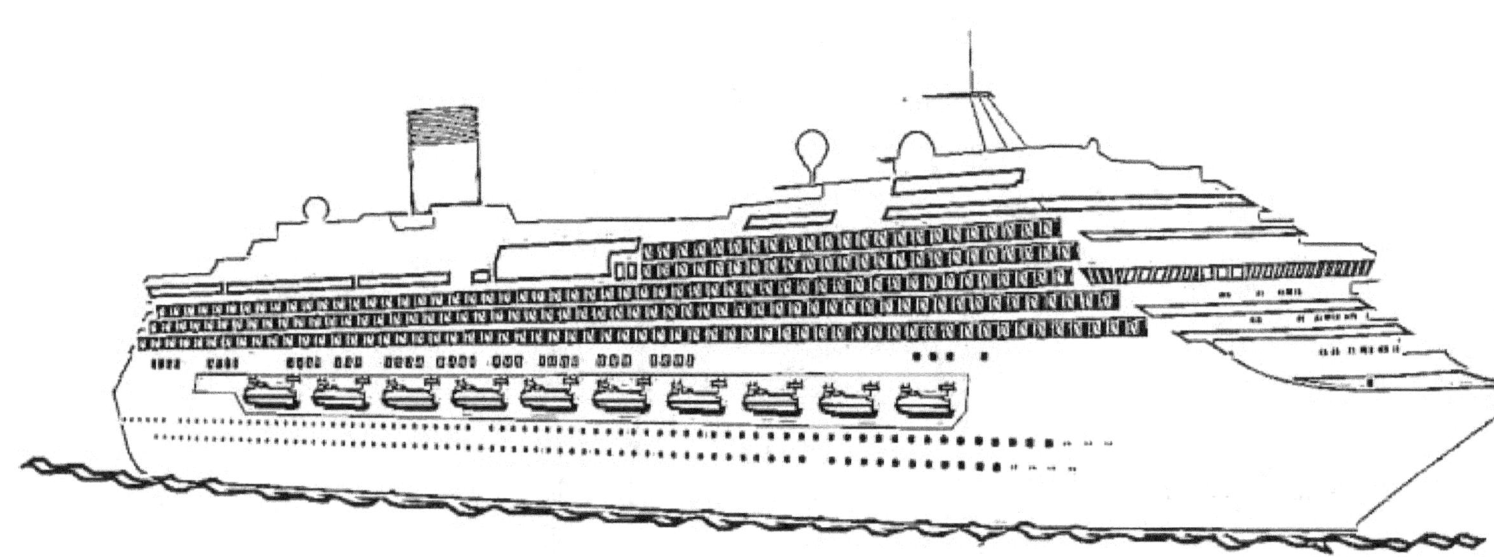

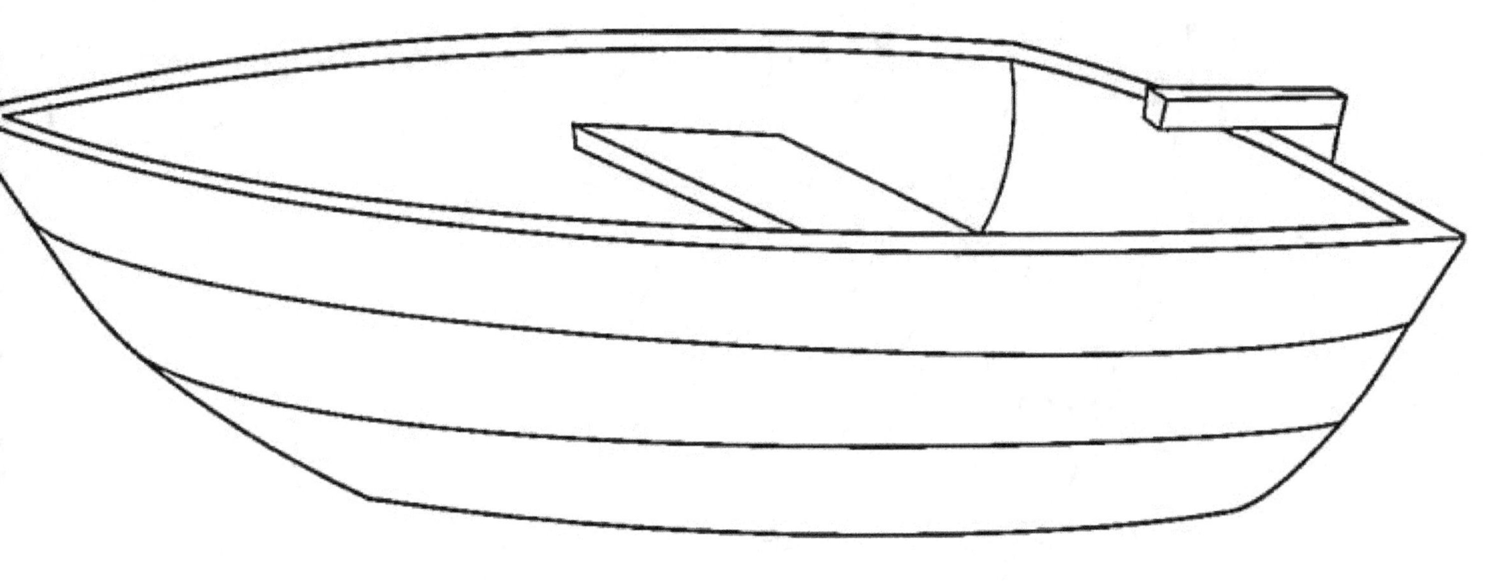

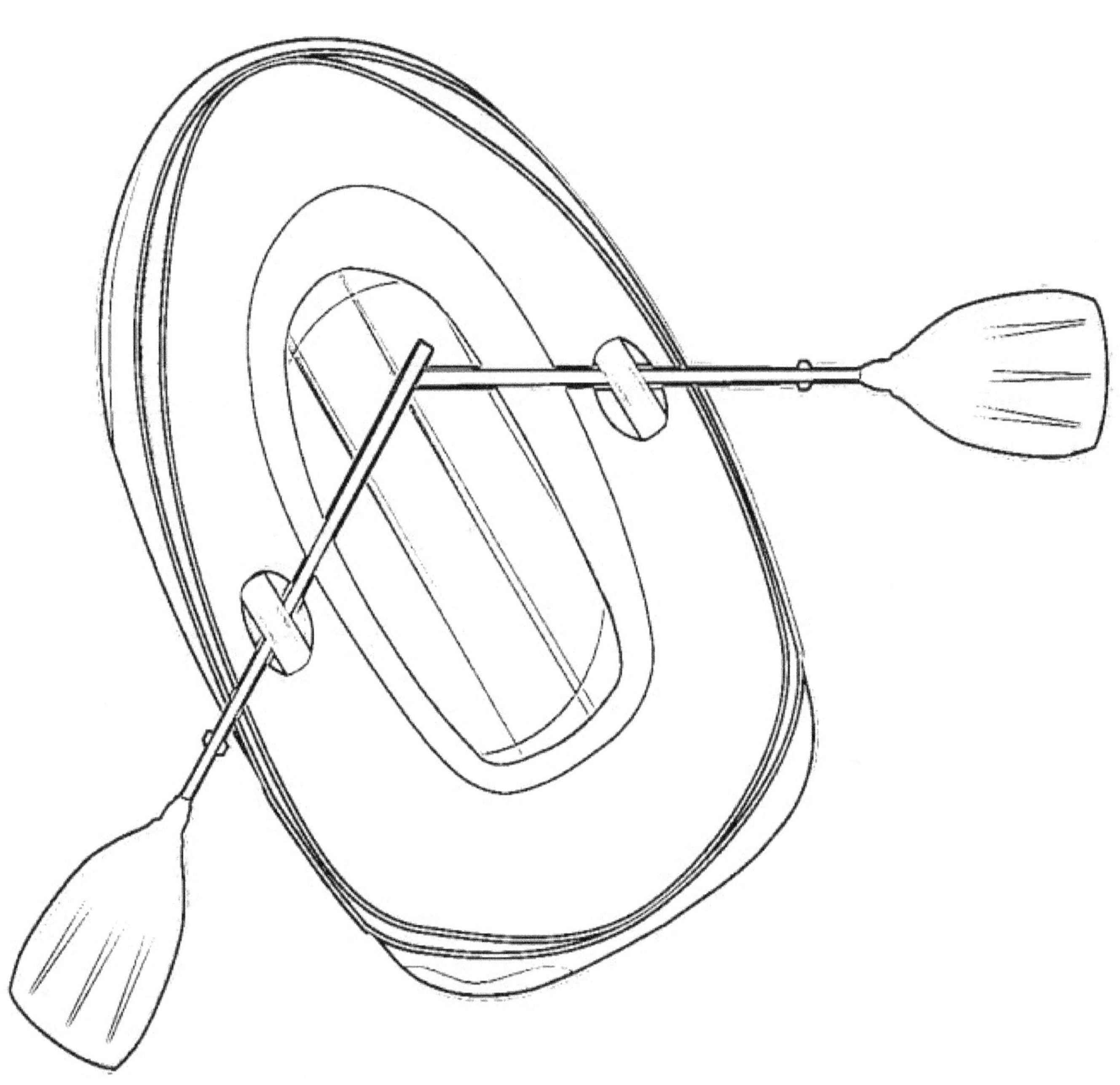

Bulldozer

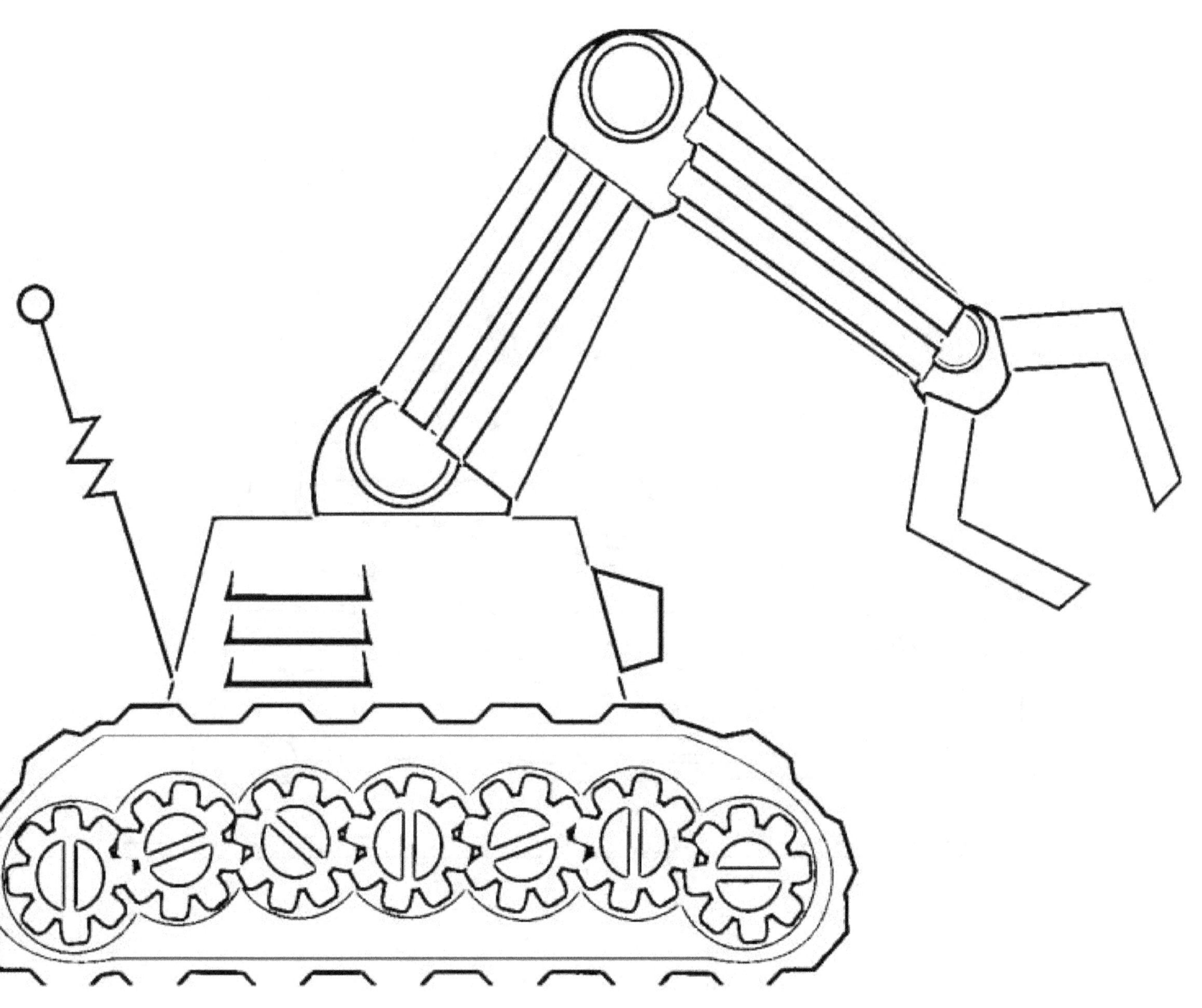

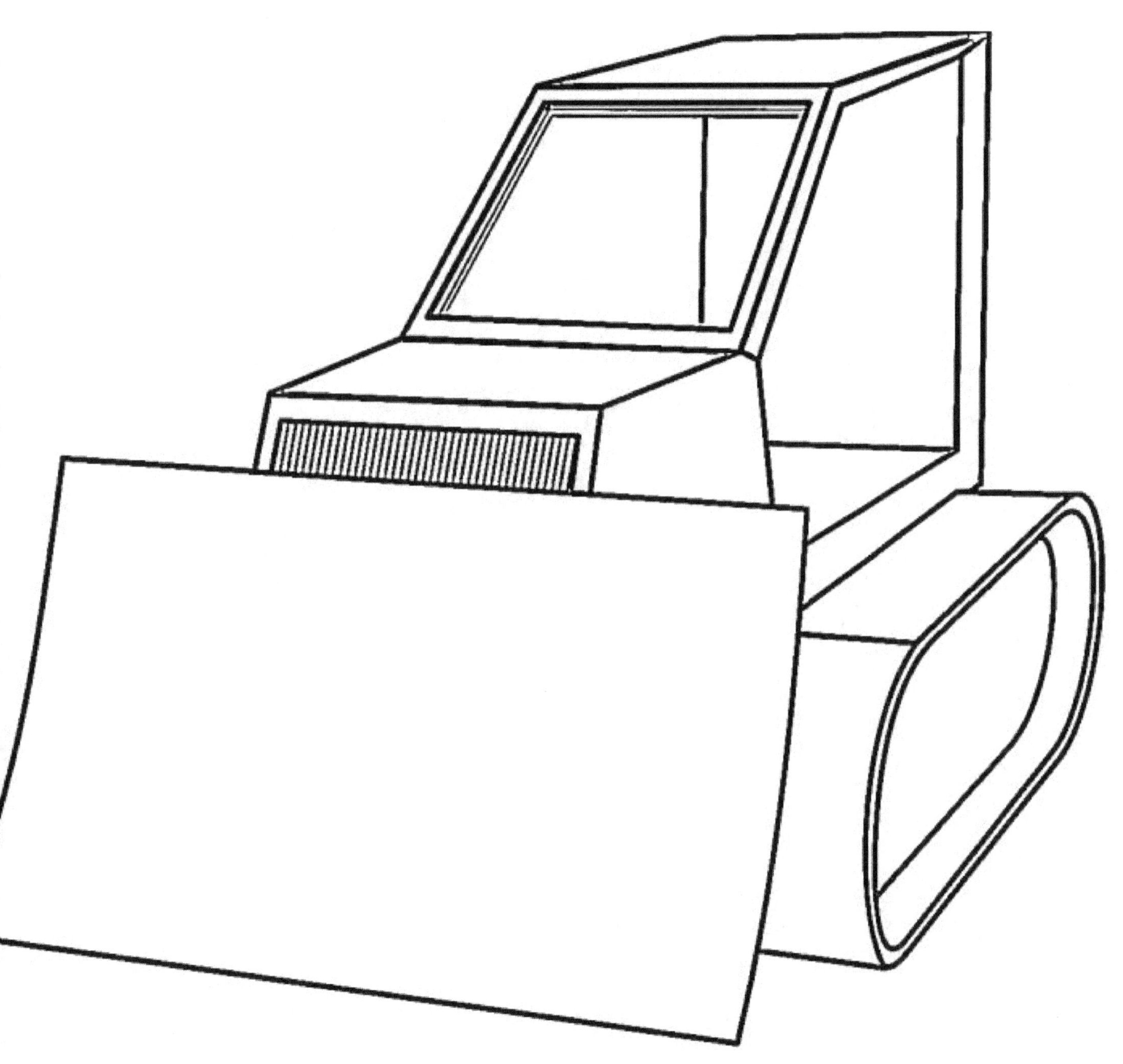

Motorcycles &
Bicycles

Piaggio Vespa 125 Sprint

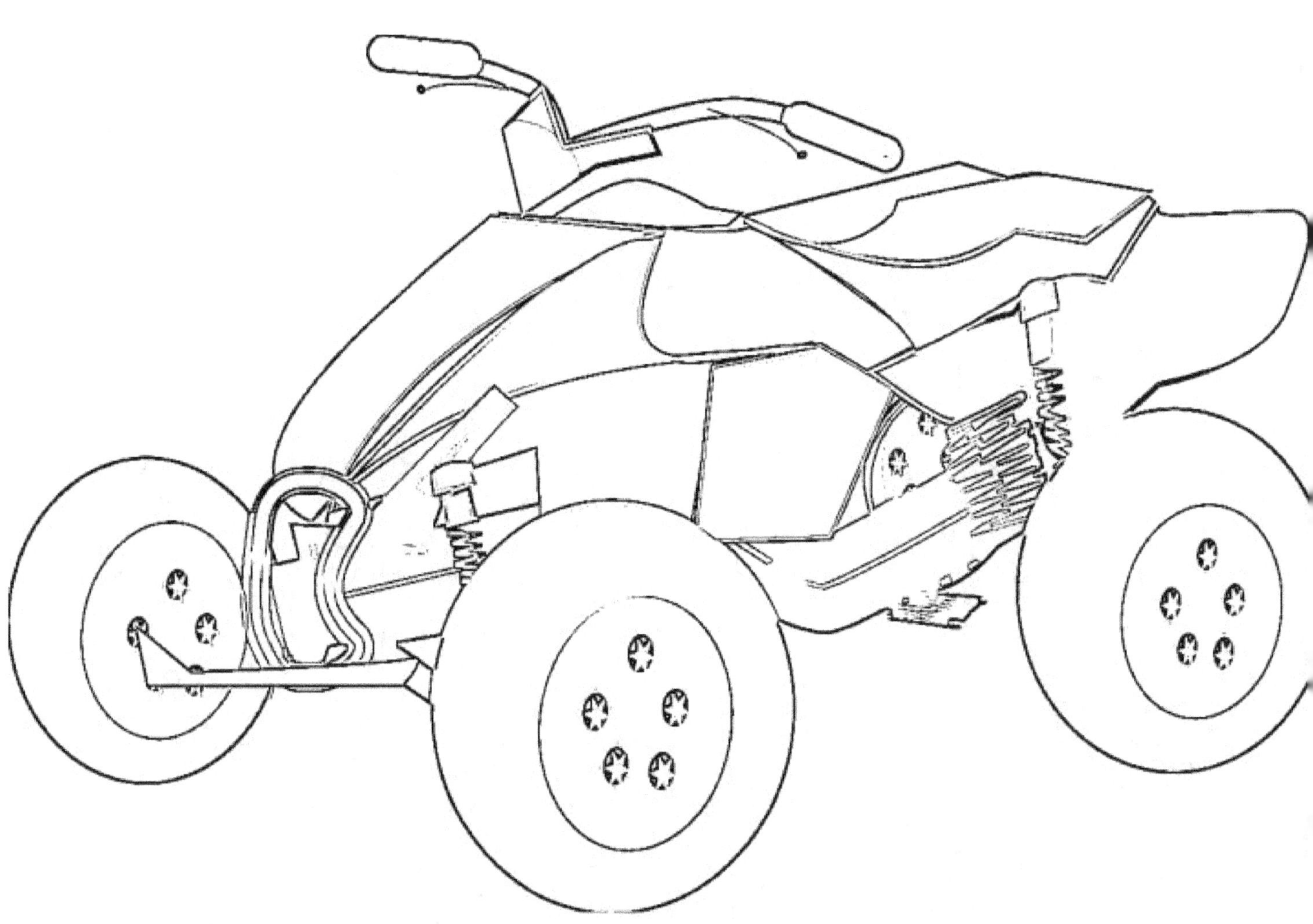

Thank You